MW00782500

WORTH OF DIAMONDS

poems based on inspired events

by
EBENEZER O. MAKINDE

MADE FOR
SUCCESS

Made for Success Publishing
P.O. Box 1775 Issaquah, WA 98027
www.MadeForSuccessPublishing.com

Distributed by Made for Success Publishing

First Printing

Library of Congress Cataloging-in-Publication data
Makinde, Ebenezer O.
        Worth of Diamonds

                p. cm.

LCCN: 2022918514
ISBN: 978-1-64146-753-7 *(HDBK)*
ISBN: 978-1-64146-754-4 *(eBOOK)*

                Printed in the United States of America

        For further information contact Made for Success Publishing
                +14255266480 or email service@madeforsuccess.net

table of contents

an up that never came down... 1

yes, you are a king 2

I hear the thunder 3

hope lamore... 4

the devil's deeds.. 5

the shell 6

dare to dream... 7

believe in yourself.. 8

lemonade... 9

shoot for the stars 10

cup of love... 11

wings... 12

dreamed a dream.. 13

my reflection... 14

glorious.. 15

blame game.. 16

love letters 17

patterns.. 18

give me a place... 19

hard to love.. 20

above the rubble.. 21

a new year.. 22

the heroes 23

circles, squares and triangles 24

purposeless people.. 25

today... 26

peace be still.. 27

champion.. 28

ten years old 30

hope.. 31

system 32

bad bills... 33

a free man's dream.. 34

what is love?... 35

veneers... 36

hats.. 37

resilience 38

hopeland.. 39

hearts & dreams... 40

growing in the dark 41

an empty mind 42

perfection 43

I would rather 44

one day 45

the river 46

consuming fire 47

success 48

hell's hit list 49

aim high 50

falling in love 51

comfort 52

transformation 53

choices 54

a new world 55

your friend 56

to the world 57

dating 59

our best 60

noah 61

wealth 62

the enemy 63

still waters 64

goodness 65

excellence 66

conquer 67

thinking 68

the devil's deeds: part 2 69

for me 70

build 71

unique 72

bearers of light 73

shepherd 74

rejection 75

singing 76

prosperity 77

power 78

strong man 79

if I was courageous 80

still 81

dad 82

fathers 83

alone 84
proud 85
beyond myself 86
heaven 87
mother 88
proud 89
me 90
hope 91
places 92
lift you up 93
the victor 94
mediocrity 95
hello world 96
stone of hope 97
family 98
help 99
leadership 100
leaders and followers 101
let us be 102
diversity 104
self-respect 105
confident strength 106
thirty years 107
for you 108
kings and queens 109
problems 110
manhood 111
God is 112
praise 113
memories 114
a house, a home 115
a blessing it is 116
contents of the heart 117
wells of hope 118
call for hope 119
soil of kings 120
the devil's deeds: part 3 121
violated 122
utopia 123
the universe 124
time to think 125
dry season 126

father's embrace.. 127
titan 128
turning our backs 129
ceo 130
silly rabbit.. 131
authentic leader 132
God class.. 133
who am I 134
the hero's path... 135
conviction 136
if I fall 138
a lovely love 139
creativity.. 140
fear & doubt 141
the crowd... 142
breathe... 143
father 144
the process.. 145
love for others 146
wellsprings 147
poison 148
fate.. 149
enthroned... 150
burn 151
extravagant 152
manifesto 153
just fly... 154
man of fire 155
immigrants.. 156
rest 157
legacy.. 158
aging 159
direction we go... 160
mastery 161
the artist 162
state of mind 163
worth 164
inner child.. 165
something greater 166
dimensions 167
deserving 168
wounds 169

mercy *170*

need mercy *171*

force *172*

living clean *173*

reshape ourselves *174*

our garden *176*

manufacturer *177*

mantles *178*

goodbye *179*

the future *180*

direction *181*

wild wild west *182*

low moments *183*

personhood *184*

trailblazer *185*

free at last *186*

kingdom *187*

I write *188*

noble cause *189*

association *190*

mandates *191*

water *192*

caterpillar *193*

only love *194*

angels *195*

mercy *196*

shine *197*

I want *198*

ankles and knees *199*

thankful *200*

in need *201*

willing *202*

the mediocre man *203*

new walk *204*

hear me *205*

real love *206*

radical *207*

mystic *208*

clouds *209*

see you again *210*

legacy *211*

power, wealth & influence *212*

city of irresponsibility 213
trouble 214
mind of the past 215
samson 216
the devil's promise 217
let me be free 218
it is written 219
cravings 220
better man 221
where dreams die 223
the way she 224
sheep 225
I need you 227
made by God 229
hello, leadership 230
divided house 231
hold me close 232
longing **more** 233
the good fight 234
a golden heart 235
the general 236
the titans and the kings 237
history 238
infinite laws 239
oppression 240
through the fire 241
agony 242
press on 243
future 244
maximizing the maximum 245
false dreams 246
diamonds 247
what's inside 248
closer 249
the truth 250
troubles 251
draw us near 252
these words 253

an up that never came down

up high in the sky, lost in the clouds
so far from the earth below,
and with my wings, I fluttered proud—
beyond my wildest dreams I go
where no dark shadows show

is it just me? imagining? an up that can never come down?
and thinking much, my eyes, they widen,
my smile soon turns to a frown.
the wind now grips me, no more renown,
my strength, I cannot confide in.

but then it came, just from the east,
a thing I could never imagine:
an encouraging word, a mighty beast,
one with great power, to say the least,
flying with fervent passion.

in one short swoop, it lifted me
raising me higher
and higher...
and higher...

to an up that would never come down.

yes, you are a king

you may have struggled with your issues,
and your temperament may swing,
you may have wallowed in your loneliness,
but still, you are a king.

do you see the crown you're wearing?
does your boldness shake the moon?
'cause you've got the deadly swagger
that will light up any room.

yes, we know the times are changing
from fall to winter and spring.
others may hate the changing seasons,
but still, you are the king.

are there wars in distant places?
broken families on the rise?
children living with no parents,
doomed to face their own demise?

if I claimed that you could save the world,
would you believe it to be true?
if I spoke of mighty power,
would you believe that it's in you?

do you see the robe you're wearing?
and that giant shiny ring?
we can hate them if we want,
but still, you are the king.

have they heard about your confidence?
or have they listened to the lies
that say that you've been silenced,
like a whimper in the sky?

from your darkest nights of failure
to the critics that so sting
yes, you stomp upon those troubles
and take your rightful place as king!

I hear the thunder

Lord, I hear the thunder
and it's calling out my name. I've been tossed around
and beaten down
but I'm winning just the same.

the disrespect
is in effect,
the reason for this heat.

there will be no lies,
no compromise,
when we meet at judgment's seat.

I've been up and down
goin' round and round,
trying to shake off all this dirt.

like I'd fallen down
and hit the ground,
trying to cover all this hurt.

yet still, I hear the thunder,
and it's calling out my name.
I'm still standing proud
maintained my ground,

yea, I'll be stomping just the same.

hope lamore

alas, I heard the knocking,
the knocking at my door,
and at once I rose to meet the man
by the name of hope lamore.

he whistled as he stood there,
basking in the morning sun.
he seemed joyful with his movements,
like a sunset filled with fun.

"why have you come?" I asked him,
knowing exactly what I'd hear:
"I came to spread some feel-good love
and make you smile from ear to ear."

it was exactly what I needed,
just a simple, cheerful word,
from the man they say could fix a room
with his sayings, though absurd.

"come in," I said, "please join me,
and we can drink some spotted tea.
I'll tell you all about my awful day
and the pain it was to me."

he looked at me, still smiling,
then with his fingers made a gun,
"I'll take that rotten day you had
and pop it til it's done."

oh, hope lamore, that's so absurd,
but I thank you for the saying.
at times in life, we all need friends
to get us through the pain.

the devil's deeds

devil: listen, my minions, please lend your ear;
we can't let that man be free,
so we'll tie him down with a mind unsound
and make addiction be his deeds.
we'll give him wealth and everything else that will choke
his heart with greed. we'll fill his cup with the lust for power,
and it'll bring him down with speed.
don't hesitate, do what it takes; just don't let his mind be free.

minions: dear master, yes, we love your plan to ruin this man's life.
we'll tie him down, we'll make him drown,
with a world that's full of strife.
we'll keep him guessing, we'll make him question,
whether our enemy truly cares perhaps before his life is done,
we'll have him binded by his fears.

day and night, with all our might, we won't let his mind be free

devil: ah, oh yes, it sounds so great,
the pain and evil, don't hesitate
to make him reach this lovely fate
where darkness and sickness so permeate
and thoughts of failure remain his state,
where the roads are rocky, and none are straight,
where the food of poison will fill his plate,
where his arrogant pride becomes innate—

a place where his mind cannot be free

minions: of course! with thoughts of shame,
we'll keep him tame and then pass
them to his seed
just watch us do it, there's nothing to it,
it'll be done by the count of three!
and if he tries to wiggle free, we'll crush him with a blow.
we'll hit him hard between the ears,

in places devils go

the shell

what is it that I contain?
is it jagged, or is it plain?

when inserted, am I the same
as all the others with my simple name

who seek to unravel this lovely game
that carries abundance, fortune, fame?

can you recall through the looking glass
the way I'm structured, the way I pass

right between those narrow ends
to a wooden thing that twists and bends
that leads to a place some may not know
a hidden land where the water flows
like dripping honey, or maybe gold?

can you tell me what I am?
for if you know the maker's plan
then soon I'll lead you hand in hand
to a place with honey, or maybe gold,
a lovely place, if truth be told

what could it be that this shell contains?
I'll whisper softly and make it plain:

it is the **key** to life. **the weak man**

the weak man stares at the pixeled screen
he slowly wipes his belly clean
with fluttering eyes devoid of sheen
he dozes off to sleep

dare to dream

for every man must dare to dream,
he must dare to conquer, must dare to scheme,
for the dream sustains him day and night
as he marches onward, with back upright,
into a sea of possibility,
a sea of peace and tranquility,
a sea of laughter, content with joy
a sea where doubt is all destroyed,
a sea where seeing can seem to see
that the diamond being polished is still yet thee
for thou art the dreamer, the keeper of plans
who draws in the future with open-stretched hands ,
and if he finds thee with eyes sealed closed,
he should not act no less composed
for the sight of this is not extreme,
for every man must dare to dream.

believe in yourself

believe in yourself and believe you're somebody.
believe that genuine meekness is better than pride.
believe that success is not measured in gold.
believe that making a difference means you're never too old.
believe. believe. believe.
believe in yourself and believe you're somebody.
believe that life has a way of righting its wrongs.
believe what you have in your hands is always enough.
believe that you'll overcome challenges, no matter how tough.
believe. believe. believe.

just believe.

lemonade

for if life gives us lemons, we make lemonade
for the debt to our past has already been paid.
by the magnificent king who once hung on a cross,
redeeming our freedom that at one time was lost.

restoring our dignity, reclaiming our throne,
as the mountains, they shudder, and the waters, they groan.
for they know of the greatness that lies just ahead,
for the lemons, once dormant, we're now drinking instead .

so grab hold of the pitcher, and pull out your glass,
and now fill up your cup with this cool drink, alas.
for if life gives us lemons, we make lemonade
and we take all our failure and we make it our gain.

shoot for the stars

shoot for the stars
and aim for as high as the eye can see
dream to the moon
and think as great as the mind can be

cup of love

whose glass is this? this cup of love?
I saw it poured from up above.
it came in spirals from way up high
beyond the reach of my focused eye
and made its way into this little glass
that till this time had been at an impasse
devoid of feeling and with little joy
for the bleeding heart in this solemn boy
but since it's here, we'll shout alas—
look at the love pouring from this glass!

wings

can you tell me? do you know?
of when my mighty wings
will grow?

not tonight and not tomorrow,
is what I think I heard you say
but do you know I'd like to fly them
somewhere in the sky today?

tell me not, with disappointment,
there is nothing I can do
for if I had such mighty wings
no doubt I'd shape the world anew.

I'd fly from house to house
mowing every unkempt lawn.
I'd wake up every neighbor
with a joyous song before the dawn.

I'd help an older lady
take her bags straight to her car.
I'd fly a group of strangers
directly straight home from the bar.

I'd fix the missing shingles,
I'd keep the chimneys clean.
I'd fly off to the mountains
all the bullies that were mean.

I'd deliver food to all the hungry,
I'd take care of all the poor.
I'd help those needing groceries
delivered directly to their door.

ah, yes, the good I'd do
if I could only grow my wings
but perhaps it's not just superman
who can do a heartfelt deed.

12

dreamed a dream

I dreamed a dream, and in that dream,
I dreamed of time with you,
and of all the dreams I've dreamed before
none other felt more true,
for in that dream, I saw you,
you were a dreamer so alive,
your giant dreaming heart was full
and it left my soul revived.

my reflection

one day I stared into the mirror
and with shock, I came to see
a hungry pompous lion
staring directly back at me:

I saw boldness in his eye,
I saw defiance in his mane,
I saw a winning growl, an attitude,
a king of his domain.

his tail was one of power
as it whipped from side to side
his claws seemed all so glorious
as they scraped the ground with pride.

I saw the things I thought I lacked
as I stared at me that day
so I bowed my head and moved along.
"I'll be someone else," I say.

glorious

the heavens shout
his glory
and the people chant his name
I think of
my past wilderness
and now I'm doing
just the same

blame game

am I the one you're blaming now for the pain that's come to be?
  it's been far too long, release the hurt, and leave it here with me.

—your past

love letters

the mailman came today, he said, "my friend, I brought some love."
he extended a tiny letter while he pointed up above. the letter read:

"what is my heart full of? **love.** so much **laughter** that, at times,
my stomach hurts. so much **opportunity** to experience new ideas
and new things. so much **victory** over my past pain and failure.
and so much **expectation** for the future—who and what I can
and will be—the man I am becoming."

I smiled as I read it as I folded it up into a perfect little square.
for, yes, my beating heart is raging full of **love.**

patterns

I'm breaking the pattern of being myself.

it's a new year and I have a new plan.
the patterns of the past determine what needs to be broken.
for enough is enough.
the up and down is enough.
I am now trusting up, and I will never come down.
I'm exiting the rollercoaster of life.

I'm breaking the pattern of being myself.

I'll never be who I once was again.
from fruit, to fruit, to more fruit, I'm becoming
more and more and more,
for I'm breaking the pattern of being myself.

give me a place

give me a place where I can rest
give me a place where I am stable
give me a place where I'm in my zone
give me a place where I'm unstoppable
give me a place where success won't stop
give me a place where demons must move
give me a place where the witches can't harm me
give me a place where I'm destined to win
give me a place where I can breathe in who I am and whose I am
give me a place where I'm at my best
give me a place where I can rest

hard to love

one way monday,
another way tuesday,
all the drama of loving you.
which one will we meet today?

one way on friday,
another way on saturday,
I'm confused on how to love you, ok?
for which one will we get today?

—all those who love you

above the rubble

I step over the rubble.
I step over my enemies,
and my walls are coming down.
I can move again, dance again, and leap again.
I am free.
I've broken from my past,
I have stepped into my destiny,
yes, I am free.

a new year

barren trees,
sprinklers blown,
shoveled snow, shoveling snow,
shoveling, shoveling, and shoveling snow.
much more snow to go.

next to the fire, hidden inside.
thoughts of birth,
but can't remember.
families singing carols, all together.
hearts breaking for the ones
that didn't make it through the year,
for the ones without loved ones, the lonely ones,
the ones alone,
(or so they think).

flight plans scheduled, some rescheduled, some delayed.
new years is approaching,
a new year is approaching.

the heroes

the ones with the courage to change their course
the ones swimming upstream against the current
the ones doing the thing that's not easily done
the ones who've faced the consequences
the ones who've escaped the prison of their problems
the quieted egos
the disruptors
the game changers
the heroes

circles, squares and triangles

in and out of seasons
inconsistency's been the reason.
circles, squares, triangles too
have been the shapes I've seen from you.

moving along these seasons in life
battling onward, no matter the strife,
hammering on to maintain his flight
yet struggles onward through the night.

dreaming of a brighter day
where the sun shines strong.

gone are the seasons of hope's delay
where circles and triangles go their way
and squares alike are held at bay.

purposeless people

purposeless people
talk about what happened
what they did to me
how I felt
purposeful people
talk about what should happen
what we should be doing
and how others feel
a shift in focus, a shift in perspective,
makes all the difference

today

today I lent a stranger a helping hand—
hell is nervous!
I took a colleague out to lunch—
demons are trembling!
I phoned my family to say hello,
now the devil is upset!
remember, the good you do for others
will be a choice you won't regret.

peace be still

when the waves of doubt, they hit me,
and the rains of pain do pour at will,
I will hear a voice behind me saying,
"my son, peace be still."

when the storms of lack oppress me,
and tsunamis of fear they thrill,
I will take my focus inward and I'll whisper,
"peace be still."

when the bills seem high,
and my hope seems lost,
and anxiety wants for me,
I'll buckle down, I'll stand my ground,
and I'll fight for peace to be.

and in the end, when I soon win,
I'll reflect upon this time.
I'll cherish all the struggles,
for through them, my peace is mine.

champion

this morning as I was lying in my bed, I heard a knock on my door. it
was an angel. he walked in and sat on the edge of my bed. his wings
were so large they
nearly touched each side of my room. he looked at me and, with narrow
eyes, said, "did you know that you are a champion?"

I waited a moment to see if there was more, but there wasn't, so I asked,
"what do you mean?"

he continued looking at me and said, "I said you are a champion.
you have impeccable **character** that leads you to do the right thing in
every situation. you are a man of **honesty,** and even if you think you
cheated someone of the smallest of things, whether it be in business or a
personal relationship, you strive to be upright in all your dealings. you
are a man of **ambition,** which drives you onward to make the world
a better place. which, I will say, the world needs much more of. and
with that ambition, you are also a man on a **mission,** a mission that
goes beyond yourself and into all of humanity. but you are also a man
of **process,** you understand that becoming all that you were made to be
takes time, and that great things aren't just born overnight; they take a
lot of focused effort. therefore, **integrity** and **obedience** are words that
also describe you well. you try your best to discern right from wrong
and strive for the former whether in public or in private. and lastly, you
are a man who **never** quits. despite all you've been through, you have a
can-do attitude, and obstacles don't easily derail you."

after he was finished, we sat in silence for a minute before the angel got
up and made his way to the door. with his back to me I yelled, "wait!"
he stopped and turned.

"that's it?" I asked, "where are you going?"

"I have a full day ahead of me, and many other lost souls need me. they
need me to show them their identity and remind them who they are," he
said.

I nodded in acceptance as I watched him exit my room and turn the corner, completely out of sight. I could hear heavy footsteps down the long-spiraled stairs and out the front door of my house.

his visit made me feel special and seen. he had a demeanor about him that was especially friendly.

a few minutes later, after reflecting on his visit, I balled back up in my bed and fell back asleep.

ten years old

ten-year-old me. innocent. protected.
pure.

soon feeling defenseless, facing life's battles on his own,
fighting to survive.
mistake after mistake, dead end after dead end,
broken relationship after broken relationship.
heartbreak after heartbreak.
he's still here, and he still stands.

strong, resolute, full of conviction, driven, hopeful.
he stands.
broken but healed,
he stands.

hope

deep mourning into dancing.
not an abstract experience,
but the face of my father shining.
we receive the favor of his face.
his grace is resting upon us.
abounding in joy
and laughter too.
my hope is revived
when I'm with you.

system

become a problem to the system.
become a problem to the game.
become a problem to the thief
that caused your heartache and your pain.

become a problem to the thought that
you, my friend, cannot be free,
that the problems that you face right now
are resigned for you to keep.

for it's time to take the offense,
time to do what must be done.
you must battle with your demons
till you come out number one.

bad bills

when I was twelve,
the enemy sold me a bad bill of goods,
telling me I needed what I didn't really need,
telling me I wanted what I know I didn't want.

and because of it
I'm angry.

so I pen these letters,
I write these words.
for I want revenge.
I will accept no recompense.

I've decided
to wage war.

a free man's dream

the anger.
burns like fire, shut in my bones.
born of confusion,
false comforts,
lies, and now betrayal.

for the friendship
with the enemy,
was never truly friendship.

and the dream
of the enemy,
I now know,
was never truly a dream,
a real dream.
a free man's dream.

what is love?

love is the feeling you get when you _____.

to be determined.

veneers

the truth is,
you're only a veneer away
from being who you always dreamed
you could be.

on the other side
of the failure
of your past
is the pathway
to your future.

so give yourself love.
don't beat yourself up,
or get hung up on the mistakes you've made,
your past regrets.

you're only one step away
from a very bright future.
in fact,
it's here now.

hats

tell me who
I was made to be.
for I've never really known.

I've spent all my time,
trying different hats,
many colors, different tones.

blue ones, green ones, black ones, gold ones
brown ones, red ones, new ones, old ones.
fat ones, skinny ones, gray ones, white ones
big ones, short ones, tall ones, light ones—
none seem to fit
my composure, posture, strength, and wit.

but if you tell me
who I was made to be,
perhaps a hat
might fit on me.

resilience

Rest assured that the
Experiences of my past have prepared me to
Stand firm through the fiery furnace of my current situation
In spite of the trials I may now face, I
Look to my father for help as I
Invite him into my circumstances and situations that are holding me back
Extending his power and influence over the
New world I'm striving to shape, minute by minute, hour by hour, day by day
Creating a better future for all who will come after me tomorrow. love,
Ebenezer

hopeland

H...
O...
P...
E...
L...
A...
N...
D...

hearts & dreams

if broken hearts and broken dreams
were ours for us to mend,
what type of tools
could we even use
to fix them in the end?

for hearts and dreams
are fragile things
for one to fix alone.
one small mistake
with a tool so great
will leave with nothing to atone.

so instead of using saws and hammers
to fix your heart and dreams,
perhaps the tools of love and peace,
will lead to better things.

growing in the dark

we do our best growing
in the dark place,
in isolation,
away from the crowds,
when we're alone.

but it isn't popular
in today's time
to unplug,
to withdraw.

to disengage,
to cover oneself
like a tiny seed
in the ground:
to be nurtured
and fertilized.

but I believe
that in this new world
it is the only thing
that will bring us back
to our sanity.

we were never meant,
to be so connected,
to find ourselves lost
in the hustle
and bustle of life.

so, like little children,
we must return
to the secret place,
where solitude
is our closest kin
and quietness,
our trusted friend.

an empty mind

a quiet mind
is a gift
that the giver gives
to those
who aren't afraid
to be alone
with their own thoughts.

perfection

perfection
can be attained
only when you realize
that under the dirt
under the dust
under the lies
remains the truth
about yourself:

that you
were already made
perfect.

I would rather

I've decided
that I would rather
live a quiet
and productive life
than live a life
chasing money
and fame,
all the while
becoming more broken,
hurt,
and degraded
devoid of peace
on the inside.

one day

one day,
we will discover
that the experts
got it wrong,
that we were never
meant to live
in isolation
from community.

for how can one
hold a hand
or give a kiss
or embrace
or hear a laugh
through the airwaves –

a place where a hug
is not really a hug
and a kiss,
not really a kiss,
but only a counterfeit
of true community.

the river

jump into the river
jump into the river

there's freedom in the river
there's fire in the river
there's redemption in the river
there's life in the river

jump in
jump in
jump in

consuming fire

how dark be the night?
how bitter the soul?
how great the desire
for the glory of old?

there's light in the graveyard,
there's still a spark in sky,
there's a hope that still burns
when the fortune seems dire.

success

I would rather be remembered
for the good I did for others
than for the things I accumulated,
for things are fleeting
and do not define
true success.

but true success
as I see it
is a deep concern for others
that affects every area
of life.

it is
the handling of responsibilities
as a father
a brother
a friend
a son
a man.

hell's hit list

just so you know
once you become
sick and tired
of being
sick and tired
and you make up
your mind
you are ready
for change
hell will put you
on its hit list
to terminate you.

aim high

nothing is too big.
nothing is too much.
nothing is too great.
no aim is too high.

think of me
and then aim higher.

sincerely,
your dreams

falling in love

do not fall
in love
with the face
and the body.

fall madly
in love
with the spirit,
the heart,
and
the character.

these are the greatest assets.

comfort

God is setting me free,
not from any particular thing,
but from the chains
of seeking
comfort
in anything
that is not him.

when I reflect back
over my life
on my past
I see that these were the chains
that kept me in bondage:

the chains of false
comforts from people
that did not care
for my best interests
and the chains of things
that were not him.

transformation

our thoughts
should not be born
of our past;
therefore,
the greatest transformation
should first come
in our head.

choices

I was never
given life
so that I'd become
a slave
to my body
using it
as merely a means
to make money
and gain
"notoriety."

though my body
is beautiful
my mind
is greater.

therefore,
I choose
to protect
my body
and strive
to use
and maximize
my mind.

in return,
I accept and welcome
the peace
this choice brings
to my soul.

a new world

the clock always reminds me
of the preciousness of time
and every time
I see it tick
I remember
that I must strive
to shape a new world.

your friend

it's amazing
how you've let something
you can neither taste
nor smell
nor see
nor hold
run, influence,
and take over
your life.

I'm flattered,
to say the least.

your friend,
the internet

to the world

to the world:
who authorized you
to build bridges
between lands
you have not crossed?

who permitted you
to conduct commerce
in markets
you have not shopped?

who allowed you
to start schools
in communities
you have not lived?

who encouraged you
to push your ideals
in lands riddled
with the bloodlines of kings?

who directed you
to act as savior
when you yourself,
have not been saved?

what power,
beyond wealth,
qualifies you
to traverse these lands?

for your twisted ideals
are not our ideals.
your nightmares of dreams
are not our dreams.

your corrupted systems
are not our systems.

your godless values
are not our values.

good intentions
are no longer enough.
we're better on our own.

dating

dear prospect—

do you realize
that nothing you've shown me
on our last three dates
has impressed me?

not your money
nor your cars
nor your super cool clothes
nor your "followers"
makes you any more
in my eyes.

I'm looking for
and needing
something much more.
something authentic.
something deeper.
something real.

our best

willing to fight to impose it.
willing to kill to protect it.
locks on your window,
chains on your door
the best government we have
isn't good enough.
a foundation built on distrust.

rule of the majority,
but the protection of the minority.
schizophrenia.
requires discrimination,
demands division,
encourages opposition,
not unity.
let us institutionalize
the devaluation of a human.

a place where
women work the same hours
and yet are paid less than our men.
a system where one hoards power
for oneself.
a system where people
are used and abused.
a place where the church and state are separate,
and yet,
we demand morality.

is this our best?

noah

sometimes I wonder
what noah felt like
when he spent day after day
building an ark
with not a drop of rain in sight.

it seems quite crazy
to prepare for something
that only you believe
will eventually come.
but...

to the noahs,
onward we build
onward we plan
onward we prepare
for the future
that we know
will soon come.

wealth

could it be
that your wealth
that you proudly flaunt
as a blessing from above
is really not
an indication
of your alignment with
his will,
but simply a byproduct
of living in the midst
of an economy
where resources
are plenty
and the opportunity
to accumulate money
is so good
compared to that
of the rest of the world?

the enemy

if I were the enemy
and I wanted to stop you,
I'd attack you with busyness.
I'd make your phone go off
and your messages blow up.
so you would become a survivor
and not a succeeder.
I'd remove every still place
so you would have no quiet place
to think from.

if I were the enemy,
I'd let so many things happen to you
along the way—
crazy kids
crazy wife
crazy marriage.

if I were the enemy,
I'd keep you full of pain
and stress
and bitterness
and anger
and unforgiveness
to distract you from being creative
and birthing concepts
that could change the world.

still waters

he leads me by
the still waters,
and he restores my soul.

he leads me onto
the paths that are right,
and he restores my soul.

he leads me by
the green pastures,
and restores my soul.

he leads me onto
plains of peace,
and he restores my soul.

he leads me through
the furnace of fire,
and restores my soul.

he leads me through
the darkest valleys,
and he restores my soul.

goodness

today I realized
just how much anger
and bitterness
and unforgiveness
I have been holding onto on the inside,
for friends
for acquaintances
and for people
who have hurt me,
whom I have not forgotten.

today, I decide that I will let it go.
I will forgive.
not for them,
but for me.
in order to reclaim my power
and my destiny.

surely,
goodness and mercy
will follow me all the days
of the rest of
my life.

excellence

the greatest gift
the pursuit of excellence gives us
is its cost.
excellence will cost us
what mediocrity will save us.

conquer

excellent people
will conquer
what an average person
complains about.
a person of excellence
chases solutions
rather than focusing
only on problems.

thinking

habits of failure
always originate in our thinking
translate into our speech
and are only then reflected
in our lives.

the devil's deeds: part 2

minions: master, what sorts of things do you see as essential
to corrupting the destiny of a human being?

devil: my wonderful servants, I search for those terrible humans who
have the most greatness locked deep inside of them, first and foremost,
of course. whoever my enemy seeks to use in a mighty way is always at
the top of my list. from there, my destruction seeks to begin disrupting
the very genesis of their life, setting them on a path of destructive beha—

minions: affecting their self-esteem, I assume, master?

devil: please don't cut me off.

minions: sorry, master. we just happened to get a tad bit excited as you
were speaking.

devil: don't let it happen again. but yes, when I sense there is greatness
inside of any individual, the attack must and will come early. my goal
is to limit any and all self-esteem that person may have. but, again,
only those who I see as making a somewhat significant difference in
the world are the recipients of my attack. all others can happily go
along their way. they are really of no
use to me.

for me

God is for me.

he is for my dreams
my desires
my goals
and my purpose.

he is for me,
in spite of my haters
in spite of my doubters
and in spite of my own
self-doubt.

he is for me.

build

true wisdom
is understanding
that I was created
in God's image,
not my own.
there can be
no greater revelation.

and with that confidence
I seek to build
the world around me
into a reflection
of myself,
my true nature,
in God.

unique

lion-like passion,
as gentle as a lamb:
the duality of true greatness,
unusual and peculiar,
unique in every way.

bearers of light

those who are called
to stand out
and are called
to be great
may be unusual people.

they may need
to be reminded
that it is usually such people
that are the chosen
to be the bearers
of the world's
greatest light.

shepherd

a good shepherd's heart
will care so deeply for his sheep
that he will leave all the others
to go after the one
because he knows
that the one
has put all his trust
in him
depending on him
and him alone
to bring them home
when he is lost.

rejection

neglect and rejection
make love seem strange
causing you to leave what is true
for what is false
and reject the authentic
for the counterfeit
and favor pain
over peace.

singing

I can hear
the angels singing,
the heavens are open,
the heavens are open

the beautiful melody
is better
than a thousand voices
here on earth;
I wish
you could hear them, too.

prosperity

true prosperity
is a reflection
of what is stirring
and blooming
on the inside.

power

thickened hair
and darkened skin
will not keep me from my win.

pressure pains us
black and white
throughout this drudging,
bloody fight.

but come the darkest
night to me
I will never bow or cower,
but thank the God who reigns supreme
for my potent,
unmatched power.

strong man

I am a strong man
who cries often
when something touches me,
who laughs often
when something makes me smile,
who fights often
when injustice stands in my way,
who prays often
when events seem out of my control,
who listens often
when I hear things I don't understand,
who forgives often
when people hurt me to my core,
who believes often
when times are tough and hope seems gone,
who wars often
when my soul's on fire and my cause is right,
who trusts often
when I'm still healing from my past,
who dreams often
when I think of building for the future.

yes, I am a man.
a strong man.

if I was courageous

if I was courageous,

I would keep quiet
and listen,

I would kneel down
and pray,

I would speak up
and share,

I would break down
and cry,

I would take a chance
and love.

still

one day,

you will look back on your life,
back to every opportunity missed
every business deal failed
every relationship severed
every hardship faced
every bill gone unpaid
every dollar squandered
every mistake made
every fear that gripped you

and you will say,
"in spite of it all,
I still conquered."

dad

today,
I woke up thinking,
I miss you, dad.
but I know you're dancing
with angels' wings
somewhere up there
in heaven.

october 8th, 2021

fathers

let us be great fathers
so that our children know that we love them.
so that our sons know that we value them.
so that our young men know that we respect them.
so that our daughters know that we'll protect them.
so that our young ladies know that we'll affirm them.

let us be great fathers
so that we can build a stronger family,
a better community,
a more stable city,
a vibrant state,
and a more loving world.

alone

I can't help but think
about the day
when I will hold my son
and teach him the things
I wish I would have been taught
and be there for him
in ways my father wasn't
there for me.

I look back
on old photos
and sometimes I weep
because I know
that I didn't know
how alone
I really was.

proud

I hope and pray
that God will allow me
to live a life
so special
so influential
that my great, great, great
grandkids
will be proud.

beyond myself

refuse to believe
that you alone are your own
hero,
that you don't need any help
beyond yourself,
above yourself,
to heal yourself,
to lead yourself.

you've been through too much.
you've survived too many battles.
you've been under too much fire.
you've been forgiven too many times
to put that weight
on just yourself

so seek something higher,
something greater
to bring you wholeness
and peace.
there is a hand
that is guiding you.

heaven

sometimes I wonder
what heaven is like
and if the best things on earth
even come close
to what it will be.
it's hard to wrap my head
around eternity
though it has been placed
inside my heart.

mother

some of my fondest memories
of comfort
as a child
come from my mother.

late nights,
tossing and turning,
waking her up,
sipping hot chocolate.

it's the little things she did
when I was a boy
that brought me comfort
and peace.

she is my mother
I am her son.
thank you, Lord, for giving me
a great mother.

proud

one of my greatest hopes
is that one day
in the not-too-distant future
I will wake up
and feel what it feels
to be authentically me
comfortable in my own skin
confident in who I am
proud of the me
that is me.

me

I want to be me.
I want to be
as authentically me
as a me can be
so all can see
what it means to be
a person of value
when I am just me.

if I could just be
the greatest me
the world would change overnight,
you'd see.

if I could be
the freest me
there's no doubt in my mind
all the blessings to be
because when push comes to shove
and the final drum rolls,
in the final analysis
me is perfect,
I'm told.

hope

hope is the substance
of things hoped for,
the evidence of things not seen.

but I wonder,
if hope was truly a substance,
evidence,
as they say,
would I find it on my fingers,
all over my hands,
somewhere in my hair?

would I find it
all over the floor,
dribbled on the sidewalk,
smeared all in the grass,
somewhere in my bed?

if hope was a substance,
would I be able to see it
hold it
smell it
bend it
fold it?

if hope was a substance,
would only few have it?
would it be considered
as rare
as many precious metals?
would it be
as common as copper
or silver?

if hope was a substance,
would anyone find it
on me?

places

there's a place I've never been.
it's a place inside my heart.
I hear its beauty is unmatched,
that it's been splendid from the start.

so I close my eyes and wonder
how great could this place be?
is it somewhere I can settle?
a place that fills my heart with glee?

as I close my eyes and ponder
this place that some call home
I fix my mind upon it
and I make my feelings known.

at once my spirit lifts,
to depths they call my heart,
and I'm filled with utmost joy
for it was *love* right from the start.

lift you up

when you know
that God is for you
it will fill you with power
lift you up, set you up high
and push you ahead
to a place
no human
can even comprehend

the victor

out of the burning ashes
from the graveyard of the soul
comes a bloodied fighting champion
a valiant warrior, as days of old.

from the pit of all despair
treads this conqueror to and fro
rising up and even higher
to heights where only victors go.

there's not a prison that can hold him
not a soul that is more bold
with defiance rising higher
to peaks that only greatness knows.

mediocrity

Meticulous planning and attention to detail are completely disregarded
   while a love for
Extravagant and
Destructive patterns become the norm, perhaps
Indicative of a society completely sold out to selfish
Overindulgence,
Complete moral depravity, useless
Religious dogma that only seeks to
Indoctrinate men and women for political gain and power,
Taking the truth and transforming it into a lie,
Yielding a society that is completely inauthentic to its core,
   unable to stand on solid principle.

hello world

hello world
it's me;
the most unique,
authentically
made human
who has ever walked
the face of this planet.

you may have never
heard of me,
but just wait,
soon you will.

stone of hope

out of the belly of the tomb
out of a bed of sod and seed
out of a town just south of jerusalem
came a king with hope indeed

out of the pages of our history
out of the books of all great men
out of the stories told about them
came our hope, again and again

out of the birthing of our freedom
out of the pain of sweat and toil
out of the blood and all the sacrifice
came our hope, up from the soil

out of a mountain of despair
out of a pit so full of smoke
out of the crevice of the ashes
will always rise a stone of hope

family

I'd give up everything
just so I could feel
what it feels like
to have my family,
children, grandchildren,
parents,
all together,
happy, loving,
enjoying
one another's
company.

—Ebi

help

our words
should always
soften a heart
turn a frown
upside down
give someone a reason
to keep fighting
provide a small spark
to brighten a day
and maybe
just maybe
help somebody
heal

leadership

so go the leaders
so go the nations
so go the leaders
so go the families
so go the leaders
so go our communities...

everything rises and falls
with leadership.

leadership is not
manipulation
or control,
leadership is something
more honorable,
something
of a higher
order.

leaders and followers

a leader
can only take people
where he has traveled
himself,
and a leader
can only take people
where he is.

therefore, if leaders
cannot go further
than the problems
we have now,
then men should choose
to follow
somebody else.

let us be

let us not be
like the world.
let us shine bright in our cities
until we shine through the darkness
and illuminate the path
to true peace.

let us not be
like the world.
let our spirits burn pure in our communities
until we burn holiness through the dark night
and radiate the way
to beholding the eyes of God.

let us not be
like the world.
let us glow bright in our countries
until we glow through the darkness
and gleam hope along the path
to finding true purpose.

let us not be
like the world.
let our talents dazzle in our callings
until we sparkle through our midnights
and twinkle like stars in the sky
on the path to our destiny.

let us not be
like the world.
let us be set apart and different.
let us hear the beat
of our own drums.

let us make our own music.
let us build our own businesses.
let us raise our own families.

let us help our own people.
let us paint our own pictures.
let us create our own inventions.

let us serve
our own God.

diversity

unity
is impossible
without diversity.
because we are different,
we can agree.

self-respect

some have decided
they have nothing to offer the world
but their bodies
and so
they've reduced their whole being
to flesh and blood,
dollars and cents,
and good lighting.

these people will do
whatever it takes
to please their senses.
they will trample,
enslave,
and prey
on the primal urges
and weaknesses of others
just to get what they want.

these people care neither
for the horizontal or vertical
planes of a complete life
and instead look out for self, devoid of any desire
for the spiritual.

power over principle.
money over morals.
crowds over character.
these are dangerous people.

there will be no hope for us
in this generation and beyond
if we cannot reach
for something greater
beyond ourselves
and hold fast to some baseline standard
of human dignity
and self-respect.

confident strength

thoughts born of our past
are often our greatest mistakes.
on the road to destiny,
there is no room
for human expectations,
shame
or guilt.

we possess
in our hands
the favor
to do exploits,
leaving behind
the destructive thoughts
that whisper, "play it safe,"
and we move forward
in confident strength.

thirty years

it's taken me thirty years
to figure it out,
but to have once been a criminal
is no mistake.

remaining a criminal
is the mistake.

for it is a dangerous thing
for a man to remain
chained and unfree.

for you

I'd cross a hundred bridges
hike a thousand mountains
swim a million rivers
run a billion miles
leap a trillion moons
just to be by you.

kings and queens

I wonder
what our world would be like
if each person internalized
the truth about themselves:
that each person
is a spirit being
of royal blood.

just as the queen is the queen,
every human is also a king or queen
and therefore
we rule here on earth.

how would we behave
if people saw us,
and, more importantly,
we saw ourselves,
as having as much responsibility
to ourselves and the world around us
as the queen?
to fulfill our call and pass the torch
to the next generation?

problems

every problem
the world faces today
can be traced back to
a lack of identity
and a lack of purpose.

we have forgotten who we are
and we don't know
why we are here.

we are lost in confusion
and abandoned in chaos.
our dreams have become our nightmares
and our minds are devoid of peace.

manhood

what does it mean to be a man?
I find myself incessantly asking this question.

I've never believed
in the fairy tale definitions
of the knight in shining armor,
of the man dominating the world and all his responsibilities,
or even the rags to riches story
of a man that has come to succeed against all odds
rising from the ashes of poorest of circumstances.

for if we peel away the neat layers
of what a man truly is
we'll likely see that the knight in shining armor
is using that armor
to hide the battle scars life has given him:
the wounds from his past,
the devils that have latched on that he has yet to master.

we may see his riches, but it's likely
somewhere on him are his rags,
the dirty rags he's used to wipe up the messes he's made along the way,
perhaps now patched up nicely and stitched into his undergarments
or maybe even tucked down deep in his socks, under his feet,
so the world can still not see.

we'll observe just above him the bar that society has created
for what success for him really means
and we will see him struggling, if he's
being honest,
with whether he can touch that standard, let alone clear it
or whether the standard even matters,
because his armor, his helmet, his shield, and his sword have now
become too much for him to carry...

and he's tired.

God is

God is
my comforter
and my caretaker
my forgiver
and my friend

he is my healer
and my helper
he's my provider
and my peace

he carries me
and consoles me
he's patient with me
and he loves me

he heals the wounds
from my past
and sets me free
so that I might live

and feel
and love
again

praise

praise
is the fuel
that ignites the hunger
the fire
and the desire
inside ordinary men
inspiring them
and like a bow
shooting them forward
to do
and accomplish
great things

memories

I know that somewhere
in the fire
are dreams fanning
to survive.

I sense that somewhere
in the water
swimmeth hope,
when hope had died.

I feel that somewhere
in the air
aspirations fly far beyond
what my eye can see,
and there's a ray of light
beyond us
illuming the path
that is to be.

I know that deep
within the night
lie visions of
a brighter day.

like the memories
in my heart,
I know they'll never
fade away.

a house, a home

when a house is not a home
it isn't that the china has not been used,
nor that the sheets have not been slept in,
nor that the floors have not been cleaned,
nor that the linens remain unkempt.

it is the little things,
the conversation at the dinner table,
the evening around the fire,
the time in silence spent in prayer.

it is the moments with family,
no matter how small,
that make
a house
a home.

a blessing it is

what a blessing it is
to be alive,
to feel,
to be able
to taste life.

let us lift our glasses
and toast
as we drink deeply
of this privilege,
to experience
every drop
of human relationship,
relationships filled
with precious dreams,
and pains
and tender moments.

contents of the heart

is it white or is it black?
is it colored or is it plain?
does its sight give off a glow?
is it polished in its name?

is it rich or is it poor?
is its value so much more?
would you tell me, if you know?
are its contents not for show?

is it faded or does it shine?
are things within it not divine?
tell me tell me if you know,
my thoughts, they wander, to and fro.

wrestling with the honest thought
should all within it be for naught?
I sit and ponder what could be
if this precious knowledge came to me.

and having wrestled to this end,
my soul, it hungers, still again.
what type of famine could this be
that yearns for such wisdom to come to me?

you may have guessed it from the start:
I want the contents
of my heart.

wells of hope

those who turn
their face to the sun
will be like well-watered gardens.

from them will spring forth
the wells of hope
that the world needs
in its time of need.

call for hope

there is a scene in a famous movie, where a rescue boat comes back after
the ship sinks. floating bodies fill the atlantic seas. the boat
crawls at a slow pace, easing its way through the bodied waters. as the
boat captain navigates the way, he cries out at the top of his lungs,
"is anybody out there? can you hear me? is there anybody out there?
can you hear me?"

it is a call for life, any life among the sea of seemingly lifeless,
frozen bodies—bodies a sudden life tragedy has made cold. but he calls
anyways, again and again, searching for some sign of movement,
a small glimmer of hope.

in the same way, those of you reading these words may be breathing,
but feel as lifeless as those bodies floating in the sea. I write these words
with a deep hunger to see you and all other shipwrecked souls fight on
in this world, and to see humanity do the same. so, I stand up, stretch
out my hand, and call out, "is there anybody out there? can you hear
me? is there anybody out there? can you hear me?" is there any life?
I hope there is still life in you to go on.

every life needs hope. every life, at times, may need a call to awaken
them to fight on. I hope these words meet you wherever you may
find yourself floating in the coldness of life's sometimes hopeless
and wearisome seas.

soil of kings

the still place,
the quiet place,
is the soil of kings
fertile with ideas
and world-changing concepts.
it requires time
and patience
with a little water and sunlight
to make it grow
into something wonderful,
a crop abundant
with hope
and love
to feed all of humanity
for ages and ages
to come.

the devil's deeds: part 3

devil: listen, my minions, and you shall hear of the reason I smile from ear to ear.

minions: oh tell us, great master, of what it could be, that pours in thine heart an abundance of glee?

devil: and tell you, I will, of the secret in me, that foresees a future that I'm fighting to be. I call my great strategy, the hope strategy.

minions: hope?

devil: yes, hope. a most wonderful and devious hope. the hope I speak of is of filling every earthling with horrible pains and agonies that will cripple their bodies and destroy their minds.

it is a hope that will completely obliterate their destinies through addictions of all kinds, creating a havoc of inner turmoil and unsound minds.

it is a hope that will destroy any sense of humility and will fill them with the desire and lust for unlimited power and influence, to do all of my other sinful deeds, fulfilling only my needs. a perfect and prosperous power with no remorse, indeed.

and last but not least, a hope of my kind will bring on a feast. a feast of great evil that is, with mere pain as the least. anything evil that your little minds can conceive, my little minions, will be the hope I shall bring. a wonderful hope that will make our hearts sing.

minions: tell the world! spread the word! hope! hope! hope!

violated

when a man has been violated
no blanket can comfort
no word can soothe
no woman can mend
no money can buy
no affair can fix
no drink can heal
no drug can cure
no vice can restore
no water can clean
the silent damage that's been done
the stain of the past
still remains

utopia

in the heart of a human
there is a longing
for something they miss,
what they lost,
a search for utopia
looking
searching
craving
for a better way.

the universe

to call God
the universe
or infinite being
or higher consciousness
is to reject
your ultimate purpose
and identity
on this planet.

it is to reject
an intimate relationship
with your heavenly father
in whose image
you were fashioned.

this is the most dangerous form
of low self esteem
and poor self-concept
because it limits your potential
and places chains on your identity.

perhaps it is a reflection
of the fractured relationship
many of us experience
with our earthly fathers.

time to think

when man cannot think,
he cannot create.
he cannot innovate.

thinking requires
time away
and time
unplugged,
devoid of the influence
of outside forces.

the man who can create
and cultivate
a space
simply to think
and act on those thoughts
in this fast-paced
technologically driven society
could rule the world.

dry season

in the dry season
you have instilled hope

in the desert
you have been my deluge

in the parched land
my downpour

in the wilderness
my rain

father's embrace

I remember
one of the last times
my dad gave me a ride
to the airport.

he didn't usually come inside
to see me off,
but for some reason
that last time
he did.

I remember him hugging me
right before I left for the gate
his embrace was stiff—
rugged—
and almost cold,
like all his emotion
was trapped
somewhere deep down
in his body.

but I could still see
the love
and warmth
in his eyes.
and as I turned to walk away,
he waited.

and I knew
in that moment
as I approached security
that he loved me
deeply.

titan

I am a titan
I am a king
I am the champion
in the ring

I am a mogul
I am so bold
I am a warrior
truth be told

this is my kingdom
this is my throne
this is my place
I'm in my zone

man of precision
man of decision
man of the first
the only edition

take charge of my future
let go of my past
no matter the times
I know I'll last

man of the fire
son of the king
ready to conquer
whatever life brings

turning our backs

let us
evaluate our past
and our potential
and, deciding firmly,
take the one or the other,
and if we choose
the latter,
let us give up
our former selves
and push onwards
toward the unpredictable,
leaving the safe confines
of lives flooded
with intimidation and fear
to ones of leadership,
the lives
we were born
to live.

ceo

to build
to fashion
to be

to master
to charter
to see

to dare
to mend
to free

to plan
to purpose
to dream

silly rabbit

s.d. rabbit made his living for many years working a blue-collar job in the factory. as the cost of living for rabbits near his garden continued to increase, and off the heels of a horrible influx of bugs who feasted on the tasty veggies in the community garden (causing many rabbits to begin living in dreaded fear), he woke up one day and decided to start making a living from working in another industry, one that no one could see, but one, nevertheless, that many other rabbits paid to have access to when they weren't digging holes in the garden or doing other rabbit things.

one day, the invisible industry was taken over in a coup by a group of terrible animals in a far away land. no one could see or hear those bad, bad animals. s.d. rabbit and many other of his friends who had quit their blue-collar jobs were now at the mercy of those wretched animals in a far away land, the ones that no one could see. because there was a coup on this invisible system, and s.d rabbit and others had quit their blue-collar jobs, it threw s.d. rabbit and his fellow rabbits to living for months in their rabbit community, sending them spiraling down into utter chaos.

then the few intelligent rabbits who had remained in the steady factory jobs, working, even amidst the sweeping changes of the times, turned to each other and yelled:

silly dang rabbit!

authentic leader

the attitude of my heart changes
with renewed understanding
and clarified purpose.
I am both
creator
and builder.

I will be, rather than do.

God class

made of a different substance,
dripping with a unique spirit
a species, one of a kind,
reflecting amazing
and dynamic qualities,
keenly aware of the maker's
original intent,
destined to fly,
filled with power,
soaked with love,
glistening with glory,
sparkling in leadership.

God class.

who am I

when you know who you are
you.
don't.
fear.
anything.

the hero's path

scale the highest mountains
climb the tallest peaks
march the winding roads
traverse the dangerous trails—
the path the hero travels,
it leads no other way.

conviction

conviction is calling the people from your past—the ones you hurt and left broken when you yourself were hurting and broken—and doing your best to make amends.

conviction is deciding you will make a living in a vocation that brings you, your family, and your future family dignity, honor, and respect, making them proud and preserving your self-respect instead of just chasing the allure of the dollar.

conviction is realizing that living and hiding a double life is really only protecting you from the opinions of other people—and destroying and tearing up your soul in the process.

conviction is having the courage to show up again and again to an environment you know is good for you, but one where you've felt awkward and alone in the past.

conviction is waking up and realizing that you are better than the decision you made the night before, even though you may not feel like there will be any consequences.

conviction is deciding that the career path you've chosen fires you up so much that you would die for it, and wanting to inspire others to do the same.

conviction is apologizing and seeking reconciliation, even when it's others who have hurt you.

conviction is deciding that you would rather create timeless and classic work—and be unknown in your lifetime—than push out mediocre work just so you can keep your content pipeline going.

conviction is the inner voice screaming to you that it's time to mature and grow up.

conviction is realizing that it's ok to be different and go against the dominating cultural norms.

136

conviction is setting boundaries in your relationships with both people and technology.

conviction is deciding to respect yourself and your body, and realizing that the most valuable things on this planet are hard to get to, difficult to find.

conviction is waking up and deciding that it's time for your life and your actions to completely change, no matter how many mistakes and bad decisions you have made in the past.

conviction is spending hours working on your craft when no one else is watching because you know deep down you have a gift, and you need to share it with the world.

conviction is making a firm decision that you'd rather feel lonely than continue giving pieces of your body to strangers, friends, and acquaintances.

if I fall

and if I fall
I will get up
and run
with the moon
and the stars
and I will be counted
as great
once again

a lovely love

if I am truly king,
my God, where is my queen?
the bone of my bone,
the flesh of my flesh,
the lover that makes me sing.

that apple of my eye,
my cherie, cherie amour,
that light of my life,
my darling indeed,
the treasure in my trove.

my honey and my sweetheart,
my dearest one, indeed,
the gal who's mastered all the world,
and yet she lets me lead,
my coco puff,
my steady rock,
the sugar to my cream,
the one whose smile
lights up the room
and whisks my mind off to a dream.

you see, a king's a king, regardless
of if he finds his queen or not,
but a love that makes him better, stronger,
is a love that should be sought.

creativity

conventional wisdom says
we must be like them
and talk like them
and walk like them
to be great,
but we were born
with brilliance
already deep inside us.

and we are now faced
with the task
of taking our buckets
and digging deep
into the wells
of our souls
and drawing from within:
new life,
world-changing inventions,
mind-bending ideas,
and fresh,
exciting,
visionary things.

fear & doubt

I am a leader.
in strength, I overcome
all fear and doubt.
I will retreat before nothing.
I will move forward
with a stately stride,
exuding the confidence
born of one who possesses
clear vision and mission,
infusing me with the courage
to press onward.

the crowd

I have freed myself from people,
therefore I
can set
them free.

a leader who needs
those he leads
to feel significant
cannot lead them,
for they will end up leading him.

one million "followers"
does not make one a leader,
for a leader is born
from internal soundness
and security.

a type of security,
that does not need
want
or desire
the crowd.

breathe

fueling my history
instead of my destiny,
thoughts of my past
think they've gotten the best of me.

events now long gone,
and the people that left,
have kept my mind flooded
with pain and regret.

holding on to what happened,
can cost us so much
so I breathe and let go,
till the future I touch.

father

I had this thought this morning, of how critical it is for our men to act as fathers, even if they do not have any biological children. whether men be in their twenties or thirties or forties or fifties or beyond, our heavenly father wants to father us, and he uses the godly men around us to do it.

my own father lived to be seventy years old, and so the men around me who are in their later years in life act as surrogates, showing a father's wisdom and love even in their older age. they show me aspects of what my father would have been like were he to have lived beyond his years.

there were many things that my father never did, or never was for me. none of us are perfect, and it doesn't mean he wasn't a good man. when I was in my teens or in my twenties, there was an aspect of fatherhood that I never received from him that my heavenly father wants me to feel and experience.

it is on me to recognize that it is likely that the man who always feels inclined to give me a hug, or to give solid, godly advice, or to put his arm around me, or to lecture me on business or personal finance, is likely acting as a surrogate, sent by our father to show me an aspect of fatherhood that I may have never received as a boy or even as an adult. this is an amazing and beautiful thing, this generational transfer of fathers that is literally built into the fabric of healthy community and family here on earth.

thank you, father, for fathers.

the process

source – images and words – thoughts – ideas – ideologies – beliefs –
  convictions – philosophies – lifestyles – destinies

love for others

if we honestly reflect
on our dislike of others,
we will be forced to ask:
why do we hate ourselves?

our negative feelings for others
is a sign of a deeper hatred
for oneself.

fall madly in love with yourself
and then you will have
a greater care
for those you lead.

wellsprings

as a leader
I am constantly monitoring
what goes into
my heart.

I guard it
and protect it,
for it is the wellspring
of my life.

I am the captain
of my ship
who leads
from the well
of the soul
that I draw from.

poison

I'll drink
the poison
and I'll wait on you
to die.

I won't
forgive you
and I'll wait on you
to apologize.

unforgiveness
is like poison
to the body
and like
a cancer
to the soul.

fate

I've always been great.
spirit so strong and
the talents innate.

success and prosperity
is always my fate.

overcome every challenge
no matter the hate.

been checking my swagger
it's been up as of late.

went shopping last night
keep my look up to date.

I've got greatness all on me
it's forever my state.

enthroned

the shackles can't hold me,
the burdens won't break me,
the tsunamis are high,
yet the waves, they can't take me.

the earthquakes, they tremble,
but hope won't forsake me,
enthroned on my heart.

watch the darkness depart,
begin with the end,
then my future you start.

burn

in the land of many lovers,
you are my first love,
my heart, my song, my time,
all of me, all of me.

you are my one and only,
I've given it all up for you.
dissect my heart,
you will find
first love.
it's you and me alone,
my bridegroom.

burn in my heart,
even hotter.
burn in my heart,
even deeper.

extravagant

welcome
as the king,
we pour out our oil
and our tears,
we anoint your feet
like the woman
who broke in the room,
the one who fell
and out came
an extravagant love.

manifesto

and this be the way
that champions train
they beat up their bodies
they welcome the pain
they callous to failure
again and again
then marvel in combat
ten out of ten.

and this be the path
that champions know
they welcome the battle
to war they would go.
hardened by contest
and so it is so
"we relish the warfare,"
their manifesto.

and this be the grave
that a champion dug
to bury the conquered,
a little bit snug,
redeeming the time,
retaking the throne,
establishing kingdoms,
and other milestones.

just fly

on the wings of the eagle, I fly
like a dove in the air, I go by
soaring and sweeping,
I'm so joyously leaping
at this moment I feel so alive.

my heart is content
though my body is spent.
reaching high in the sky,
oh, this is my bent!

so come on and fly
watch our troubles go by
oh, the places we'll see
so come along with me!

and we'll spread out our wings
and just fly.

man of fire

I peered into the furnace
and I saw a man of fire.
I could sense that only freedom
was the hope of his desire.

his arms were steel and rugged
as he held them to the sky,
a man longing to be rescued,
not abandoned, left to die.

his eyes were flaming torches,
his feet were black and soiled,
but his heart was beating stronger
than a thousand others could.

his mind was firmly fixed,
though the flames were all around
he kept his poise
and his composure
and still his crown remained unbowed.

how could this man of fire
stand to suffer all this heat?
he'd decided many trials ago
to taste victory,
not defeat.

to press onward,
not retreat.

immigrants

off to the states
in '88
another country
altogether.

our afro culture
like a vulture
kept the accent
thick as ever.

shipped from the wild,
they say and think.
my darkened people,
we all know better.

our life was good,
yes, even greater,
in the land
of tropic weather.

rest

abused and battered,
he felt scorned,
yet he kept his head
held high.

like a fighter
lost in battle,
his soul was fighting
to survive.

the glitz
and glamour,
his abundant wealth
on display for all to see.

a failed attempt
to hide the pain
and his lonely
misery.

the world saw muscles,
a shiny grin,
and a man dressed
in all his best,

but beneath all of those
flashy things
was a man
just wanting rest.

legacy

let us pray
that marriage becomes
cool again.

when you turn fifty,
your hair is graying,
your waistline is protruding,
your chest is sagging,
you've had
your "fun."

but soon then realize
you've wasted
your best years
chasing pleasure
instead of legacy,
stability,
and family.

all the while dimming
the light on your purpose
and destiny.

aging

one of these days
I might just go gray
and the hair I've enjoyed
may just fly, fly away

might get a wrinkle or two
a few crows with my winks
perhaps bags near my eyes
like I'd not slept in weeks

oh, the wonders of aging
cannot be all that bad
I'm just happy I'm living
yes, for that, I am glad

direction we go

it is our thinking that determines the direction our lives will go.
the most powerful thing a human has in his possession are his thoughts.
therefore, the source of the information we live by must constantly
be monitored and kept in check. beware of who you allow access
to your soul. constant repetition becomes the tool that can alter
our state of mind, whether for good or evil. it determines
our ultimate destiny.

mastery

self-control
is what is mastered
in the wilderness.

the artist

there was once a master artist
who began to cut and carve.
he worked all through a slab of wood,
but my God, the work was hard.

day and night he carved away,
to chisel off the bad,
perfecting its impurities—
what an opus would demand.

his feet were tired,
his arms were sore
but to cease the man would not,
for he knew behind that slab of wood
was the perfection that he sought.

then one bright and lovely day,
he found his work was done,
for the slab he'd worked so hard to shape
stood there glistening in the sun.

just like the artist came to see
and just like you and me
the work to chisel,
to shape our lives,
is a work that needs to be.

state of mind

he is what he is by virtue of the state of mind with which he identifies.
he must choose either bondage or freedom.

worth

someone tell me why
I had to go through
what I went through.
why I was chosen,
not for greatness,
in my developing years,
not for leadership
during my elementary,
not for any accolades
or awards
that would distinguish
that season
from those around me.

instead, the greatness
was one of pain
and isolation
and loneliness.
I was chosen
as the carrier of feelings
of abandonment
and I received
only the accolades
of my imagination.
I was handed the trophy
of rejection.
I was seen as great
only in my own mind.

inner child

as we age
we begin to realize
that the little boy
or the little girl
deep inside us
chose to remain a child.
embarrassed by being seen
as immature
or lacking in social etiquette,
we bury that inner child
underneath our schedules
goals
responsibilities
and plans,
hoping to measure up
to the other "adults"
around us,
"grown-ups"
who are too afraid
to embrace
their own inner child.

something greater

the day
you become forgiving
is a greater day
than when you
were forgiven.

dimensions

the heart
has dimensions
that only get explored
in time

deserving

you don't get
what you deserve
you get
what you could never earn

wounds

you don't have to hurt
from the bondage
and wounds of your past...

mercy

the dimensions
of mercy
flow from
the very heart
of God.

need mercy

the mercy
and the love
of our hearts
must spill
into the social sphere
of our world

force

forgiveness
is the most powerful
force,
for it changes cities
and nations.

it brings tyrants
and dictators
to their knees.
it brings justice
to the oppressed,
and it sets the captives
free.

it is the light in the darkness.
it is the small heat in the cold night.
it is the silent hope
of the afflicted.
it is the cry
of the weary heart.

living clean

we will never
reach our potential
if we do not strive
to live a clean life.

our future
demands a vision
that will keep us focused
and on the right path.

reshape ourselves

it is a tragedy to watch
what has transpired
with our youth.

we've given up principle
in favor of passion.
we live with no purpose
other than
to make a living,
rather than
to make a life.

we are slaves
to unrestrained pleasure,
seeking to satisfy our cravings
at all costs.
few possess self-control.

we've forgotten the security and benefit
of real love.

we either have forgotten,
or don't care at all,
about the generation to come after us.
what they will see,
how we will be remembered.
we blindly accept everything
that the systems of the world feed us.

but if the guilty must stand,
I stand first
with arms raised,
for my hands were once stained with the blood
of these very things.

but the beauty of life
is that we can decide

at any moment
to reshape
our way
again.

our garden

we open up
the gate of our soul
and welcome you
into our garden.

we beckon
your sweet presence.
we wait
for your love.
we honor
the gentle breeze
of your voice.

you are the air that we need.
our hearts yearn for the song
that you sing.

manufacturer

many people claim that the goal in life is constant improvement. "to become the best versions of ourselves," they say. "to reach our ideal state," they teach. but what is our best version? what is our ideal state? and how do we know if we are close to achieving it?

the end is not merely to become more free or more healed, for that alone is a selfish end. man was never created broken, to live a fractured existence. he was created in the mind of the manufacturer as whole, intended to be whole, and that is his normal state. therefore, his end in life must go beyond just healing.

healing is a necessary step to get a man back to the starting line, but the manufacturer, the creator of the product, is the one who gives purpose to the product. it is the manufacturer who backs the warranty, enabling the product he created to function again as intended, for its intended purpose. even if the product does not malfunction, if the product does not know the manufacturer's plans as outlined in his initial intentions governing the product, then the product is at high risk of being used and abused for the wrong purposes. that product will not reach its ideal state or the best version of itself, simply because it is out of alignment with the purpose for which it was created.

mantles

you must believe
that you carry a mantle,
to cause great things to happen.

when the favor of heaven
aligns with the favor of man
your mantle will fall.

yes, you carry a mantle.

goodbye

one day it may come
where we'll bid our goodbye
when our souls will depart
and with wings we will fly

but what will we take
on the day that change comes
when the breath leaves our bodies
and our earth work is done

will we hoard all our money
and our treasures of sorts
will we latch onto beauty
or our five-star resorts

will we carry off food
that we'd stored up to eat
will we take all our music
or our comfortable sheets

what things will we take
when we bid our goodbye
I pray peace for our souls
is the thing we will try

the future

I am a leader
who does not live for me
but for those past and ahead
who will soon come to be.

those I'm tied to through purpose,
I build on the past, and I
build for my future.

direction

with direction
we put off
distraction

wild wild west

when I was younger
we had to visit the library
to have access to the world
of information.

it was much harder to be exposed,
to be deceived,
by propaganda
and false information
simply because we had full control
of what we accessed.

we had accountability.
the library was a family endeavor.

in today's world
this is not so.
I wonder why
we don't we put the same effort
into protecting and giving access
to the internet.

perhaps we should treat it like
our libraries.
this way, we are training the next generation,
our children, to
believe that it
is a tool to be used for work
and wholesome pleasure, in moderation.

it was never intended to be handled
like an all-you-can-eat buffet.
too much of anything is not a good thing.

low moments

we do our best growing
at our low moments.
we do our best growing
in our darkest seasons.

personhood

whatever the moment,
in spite of the season,
become the kind of person
who can be trusted
with success.

trailblazer

upon this rocky way I walk,
my legs they sway and quiver.
yet I focus my attention on
a future so much bigger.

no eye has seen
no ear has heard
the dream I now pursue.
so I walk this rugged path alone
a trail for one, not two.

the people laugh
I hear their jeers
they revel in their fun.
and yet they do not fully know
this journey I've begun.

the course I trek
is untraveled road,
and peril seems to circle round.
but I know a trail in back of me
burns afresh upon the ground.

free at last

I remember
last november
all the ruckus and the crowd,
the voices in my head were screaming,
my soul was yelling loud.

I knew that I could not continue
to march on, though I could,
for I'd come to the concise conclusion
that this pressure was not good.

my heart was pounding
as I fixed my feet
and raised my voice aloud,
my God, my God
remember me!
your son of whom you're proud!

then I waited in the silence
that november morning day
as the wind was blowing
and birds were chirping,
yet my pain remained to stay.

but after time as time continued,
I felt a newfound rest.
a different feeling,
a blessed healing,
a peace stirring in my chest.

it was then I knew
my soul, it grew
and I'd been freed from all my past.
and in that moment I had to whisper,
my God, I'm free at last.

kingdom

the kingdom of God
goes much deeper
much further
much wider
much higher
than any religion

I write

I write for the individual
who quietly dreams.

I write for the dreamer
with a passion for greatness.

I write for the dreamers,
who silently hope
of doing something significant
with their lives.

I write for those dreamers,
who have yet to believe
that anything and everything
is possible.

noble cause

ask yourself,
is my life driven
by a passion
to complete
a noble cause?

association

a lion
will become a sheep
by association.
it is a crime
to lose yourself
in favor of
the influence
of the crowd.

mandates

mandates built
on human flaws
will shape a world
through unjust cause.

water

you are
the water for my spirit
so tell me what you're like—
what you love
what you see
what you dream.
change the way I think forever.
promise that as I walk
through the dry place
you will sustain me.

caterpillar

from caterpillar
to butterfly—
the transformation,
it spells the eye.
from crawling gently
to soaring high
there's not a one
that can deny
its wondrous wings
do mesmerize.
yes, the magic of
the butterfly.

only love

you are not
what you've done;
you are not
what has happened.
only love has the power
to tell you what you are.

angels

there must be angels all around me,
I can feel them in my room.
the slightest touch,
a wisping breeze,
are the ways they choose to move.

I can hear them in my chimney.
I can sense them at my door.
I can feel their lasting presence,
it always leaves me wanting more.

and I know that their protection
aids me when I come and go,
so the peace I feel inside me
fills my cup and overflows.

I have heard they have such mighty wings,
that will flap from side to side,
I have heard they have a beaming glow
like the heavens where they reside.

yes, there are angels all around me
and I can feel them in my room.
so I rest my head, when in my bed,
knowing morning will come soon.

mercy

today I've chosen
to drop my superficial power.

the prophetic act
that the world is waiting for
is the dropping of stones,
the act of becoming vulnerable,
and the release of absolute power
for influence.

it is an act of vulnerability,
of mercy,
and of dependency.
it is every ounce of unconditional love.

this will be the prophetic act
that will bring the world
to its knees.

mercy, mercy, mercy,
will win the day.

shine

shine on me
and favor me.
lift me before
the throne of grace,
for I am weary
and in need of rest.
I take my power.
I snatch it back
from the wounds
that have tried
and tried
and tried
to control me.
there is nothing
in this world
that can change
the power
of who I am.

I want

I want to love
like you love.

I want to bless
like you bless.

search me
until you know me
and set me free.

ankles and knees

I give you the keys,
for I am willing
to embrace mystery,
if it means
knowing you.

what's right or what's wrong,
I often don't know.
I was up to my ankles,
now up to my knees,
but to fully get in
to the river that cannot be crossed,
I know that I
must let go.

shape me and lead me
into the truth
and set me free.

thankful

I am thankful
for the healing tears
that flow.
I am thankful
for the stirring
in the deep reaches
of my heart.

in need

I am in need
of forgiveness,
for I am tired
of hiding.

wash it
all away.

wash the guilt
all away.
the shame,
the trauma.
all away.

you know I was deceived,
for that is why
I did it
in the first place.

I can't hide from you
any longer.
see what you
have already seen.
hold me and love me,
comfort me
and help me
also to forgive.

bless them,
and set them free.

willing

I am willing
to embrace history
if it means
knowing you.
take my past
and set me free.

the mediocre man

he is in love with meaningless things
meaningless actions and meaningless deeds
meaningless spending
and meaningless creeds

he is in love with wasting his time
wasting his energy just waiting in line
wasting his talent and
wasting his mind
he'll destroy it with things that, in seeking, he finds

he is in love with pursuing those things
that provide him with pleasure but
devoid of the things
that leave a great legacy and point to the fact
that he loved more than him,
an incredible act!

he is in need of another fix
a fix of the tv
a fix of a drink
a fix of his phone,
for a like or a wink
a fix of the club life
a fix for some sex
another new girl
he'll just end it through text

he is a man with a broken heart
a man with no confidence
right from the start
a man with no vision
a man with no goals
a man who cares less
for other men's souls
a man without action
a man without plans
a man who's considered
mediocre and bland

new walk

may not have been pure
but I'm challenged today
to guard my eyes
in an exceeding way

to live so wholly
to walk so clean
to renew my mind
to make it pristine

I am my own man
I have mapped out my dreams
I will captain my ship
I will head up my team

I had failed many times
success had been short
I'd been drug through the mud
like a rag doll of sorts

but there isn't a man
who can fix this but me
so today I walk pure
knowing I am set free

hear me

hear my cry,
harken
when I call,
attend to the longing
in my soul.

listen, and hear
the anguish in my prayer,
look, and see
the crimson in me.

remember the pain
I have endured
and recall my many
wilderness years
in the dry place
when I was lonely and weak,
wounded by life.

for it was you and I
who fought through the storm.

and now
I need you again.

real love

my heart, it skips
so suddenly,
might jump a beat—
or two or three.
my soul has longed
for love, you see,
in need of comfort
to fall on me.
and in this moment
I feel some hope
for nothing grand,
of smaller scope.
just something simple
for me to feel—
I want a taste
of something real.

radical

they say I'm
radical and ruthless
like I'm some
monster running toothless

they say I'm
tenacious and a fighter
like I'm a
fomenter or inciter

they say I
don't play by the rules
or choose to
abide by foolish ways

but regardless, I do know
that they'll be
begging me to stay

they say I'm
a gangster and a havoc
like I'm some
robber baron maverick

they say I'm
a cold and brutal killer
like I'm
a werewolf from the thriller

they say I'm
harsh and half abrupt
like I've
been living life corrupt

but despite the lies they say
I choose to walk my path
my way

mystic

I clear my thoughts
I settle down
a busy schedule
cannot be found
demanding meetings
nowhere around
my head is clear
no single sound
I take my pen
begin to write
the world in me
that's out of sight
I'm hoping for
a life so still
a life that fights
against my will.

clouds

all those mornings,
I do remember,
the sun was bright,
yet dark as ever.

and, yes, the pain,
it was so clever,
it'd come and sit,
to me it tethered.

I'd lay all day
and try to feel,
I'd ask the darkness
"let's make a deal
for a glimpse of light
is all I need.
I'd like a chance
to live and feel."

then darkness turned
and said to me
"I'll give a tease
of what could be."
then he departed
for another day.

then light beamed in
and I could see
dark clouds were lifted
from over me.

but something great
took place soon after—
the light, it poured,
much stronger, faster.

and then a whisper,
it spoke to me—
"those clouds are gone
no more to be."

see you again

I stop, and then
I think of you.
a minute passes,
then maybe two.

the thoughts of you,
now all I know,
'cause even dreams,
they never show
the part of you
I miss the most.

your presence was
the thing to me
that made my life
all it could be.

so till that day
we meet again
I hope that I
can make it through
a world that misses
the life in you.

legacy

what type of life
will I lead?
what lasting legacy
will be my seed?

was I a shaper
of other men
or did I take
until the end?

was my heart
for those in need?
or were my days
consumed with greed?

did my purpose
remain steadfast?
or did I quit
before my last
and final breath
upon this earth,
short of reaching
all my worth?

let me wrestle
with these thoughts,
for wasted time
cannot be bought.

let me wrestle
with these things,
I long to grasp
all that life brings.

power, wealth & influence

how much power
could I obtain
without it making
me seem vain?

what type of wealth
could I beget
before it feeds
thoughts of regret?

what type of influence
could I gain
before it appears
it's all my aim?

how many things
could I consume
before I run dry
of vacant room?

how big of barns
could I raise
before my possessions
become the praise?

how much of life
could point to me
before men realize
I was never free?

sincerely,
the ego

city of irresponsibility

welcome to the city of irresponsibility, a place where each citizen takes part in spreading the blame for their choices to something or someone else. here you will find—

we blame
the government
for our unemployment
alcohol
for our drunkenness
our wives
for our cheating
our husbands
for our depression
our culture
for our obsessions
and our enablers
for our addictions

if you're lucky, you may also find—

the black man blames
the white man
for his predicament
and the white man blames
the black man
for his predicament
the poor blame the rich
for their poverty
the criminal blames society
for his misbehavior
and the sinner blames
the preacher
for his perdition

we hope you enjoy your stay in the city of irresponsibility. just remember, it's never your fault!

trouble

when we choose
to shift responsibility
for our own behavior
to the society we live,
we are in trouble.

mind of the past

nothing is worse
than living
in the present
with a mind
of the past.

samson

so let him die,
with the philistines!
for they've snatched his soul
and gouged out his eyes.

for man's vision holds
the sacred key
that unlocks new worlds
and brings things to be.

but if man cannot
see where he aims,
he will toil all night,
but it will be in vain!

so let us pray,
that his sight will be,
that beaming light,
the world might see.

the devil's promise

my home is real hot;
it's the place to be.
so all of you people
come hang with me.

there isn't a thing
I can't give to you.
come ride with me
I make dreams come true.

I promise I'll give
you fortune and fame,
I'll offer the things
that will drive you insane.

yes, that is my promise
from me to you,
but I'll hide it in language
like "freedom" (it's true).

so drink of my cup,
yes, sip of it now,
and take to your knee,
yes, bow it on down.

remember my promise
from me to you:
I'll make your life great,
I'll make your life wild,
just do as I say
my orphaned child.

your friend,
s.l.

let me be free

so let me be free!
that I might
run with the wind
and shine with the stars
and dance with the wolves.

let me be free!
and I will
reign with the kings
among other things
for such great opportunity
is what liberty brings.

so let me be free!
until the bell tolls
for all of the things
that dire pain on earth brings,
like death and destruction
and internal dysfunction.

let me be free!
until shackles are gone.
midnights no more
till my soul has been mended
and is whole as before.

for freedom is found
not in a thunderous sound
nor in a flash of great lightning
or in the might of our earth's kings.

but freedom is found
in the still quiet sound
that whispers us on
when our heart's hope is gone.

"continue, my son,
for you are captive no more.
I have called you up higher.
you have so much in store!"

it is written

it's already been written,
etched in stone,
put to bed,

what the spirit has proclaimed
will come to pass
in the end.

no sense in striving to make it to work,
to force my will,
to make life bend,

no point in joining all the hustle,
the useless effort,
the culture's trends.

for the father had it written
before the supple hands of time,
he marked it up in heaven

before a day on earth was mine.

cravings

the cravings of my soul
with all their longings take their toll.
all I want is peace and rest.
save me from this horrid test.
things that fight for my desire,
a bitter war that has transpired.

guns a-blazing with their might
cannot save me in this fight.
I need a power not from earth
to wage this battle
and fix this hurt,
to mend the broken,
seal the pain,
and raise my weary
soul they maimed.

come now, father.
rescue me
from all the horror
my eyes have seen.

better man

I do realize—
and take heart
in the fact—that I am
a better man
than I was yesterday,
that I am stronger,
more disciplined,
a better lover,
a steadfast father,
and a better friend
to all those around me.

I do realize
that in this world
and in this life
there is so much brokenness
and pain
and hurt
that has fractured our hearts,
tainted our souls,
and crippled
our esteem.

but in spite of all of this
I do realize
that, day by day,
hour by hour,
minute by minute,
I am becoming
and choosing to become
the type of man
that my heavenly father
created me to be.

I do realize
that I am not perfect.
I do realize

that I can be better.
nevertheless,
I do realize
that in spite of all of my shortcomings
I was still created
perfect.

where dreams die

if dreams did die
where would they go?
somewhere near?
maybe far?
I cannot guess.
but do you know?

would they skip to the moon
or hang from a tree
or bury themselves
in the ground below me?

would they shoot up with wings
that would help them to fly
well above earth
in the sky way up high?

would they be placed in a box
and folded up tight
where no harm could befall them
through the long dreary night?

it's so tragic to think
that our dreams may just be
the reason men die
with no hope left to be.

the way she

the way she walks
and the way she talks
the way she moves
and the way she rocks
the way she comforts
the way she sways
the way she whispers
my mind's ablaze

the way she's quiet
the way she plops
the way she cuddles
my God, don't stop

the way you banter
the way you scream
the way you sleep
the way you dream
the way you heal
the way you deal
the way you cook
your favorite meal
the way you hope
for days to come
I know there's not
another one

sheep

when the sheep
have no shepherd
there is chaos
in the ranks.
there's anxiety
and depression
that will not leave
nor give concession.

when the sheep
have no shepherd
fear continues
its progression
the people's toil
hath no regression.
the young, they live
with no intention.

when the sheep
have no shepherd
evil runs
its rampant reign,
people fight
for little gain,
others die
or go insane.

when the sheep
have no shepherd
we must ask
is this humane?
is it us
to take the blame?
who would approve of
this ugly game?

when the sheep
have no shepherd

what we need
is a man to lead,
to wield his staff
till all are freed,
to raise his voice
and speak the truth
to all the old
and all the youth.

I need you

I need you
like coolness in summer
like pancakes need butter.

I need you
like sugar needs tea
like sun shining on me.

I need you
like deserts need rain
like old thoughts with no pain.

I need you
like an athlete needs rest
like school days with no tests

I need you
like coffee needs cream
like the top guy on the team.

I need you
like people need air
or like diamonds, so rare.

I need you like
a hot summer breeze
like a warm fuzzy squeeze
like my spirit needs care
like the wind in my hair.

just let me
be needy
I'm not trying to
be greedy
I just know
I'm my best
when my soul

is at rest
and the thing
that my heart needs
is you.

made by God

I was not
just made by God
but I was drawn
from his very nature,
his very essence.

I am his statue
his image
his copy
I carry
his perfections.

hello, leadership

my name
is leadership.
I am
your desire
and your destiny,
your longing
and your passion,
the instinct
deep inside you.
I'm at
the heart of
human hearts.

divided house

a house divided
cannot stand,
but a heart in two
can be made new.

a mind of many
cannot please any.
throw off the old,
embrace the new.

reshape our thoughts
to those of you.

hold me close

I'm better on your shoulders
could you hold me?
it's getting colder,
I just need a single touch.

it's not a lot,
it isn't much,
but if you're willing,
pull me tight,
take my hurt and make it right.

the trauma had me,
oh, yes it did.
the dirty stains I could not rid.

wash me clean,
then hold me close.
I need your comfort
and love the most.

take my hand
and squeeze it tight,
tell me that I'll be alright
even in
this lonely night.

longing more

purify me
make me clean
so my shameful past
can be redeemed.

I was so lonely
when I did those things—
such weighty bondage
is what they bring.

I cannot carry
these bags no more,
a better future
I hope is in store,
for my heart is truly
longing more.

the good fight

my father—
your legacy lives on.
you were kind to a fault
and we owe you a debt of gratitude.

your personal touch,
the presence you carried,
your life was a blessing,
your memory a treasure.

though you stomp no more
your tremors remain,
a living testimony that you came,
you fought a good fight,
and you left
an indelible mark
on the sands of time.
may the grace of God
numb the pain
of those you left behind.

a golden heart

a golden heart
stopped beating.
you were a gift from God
and now you are safe above.

though our love was dear,
we could not make you stay,
in this it's proved
that God only takes the best.

the road was getting tough,
the hills were harder to climb,
so you were called home.

it breaks our hearts to lose you,
but we gain solace in knowing
that you are in a better place.

kind and true,
we could always count
on you.

you were one in a million.

the general

outstanding general
a leader
from the front
bold, fearless,
and unmovable
a soldier in every sense
unbendable
in matters of truth
tough as steel
but willing
to sacrifice it all
to help the helpless,
all those in need

the titans and the kings

the rulers of the world
and the undisputed kings
mighty and dynamic
destined for the greater things

the masters of the universe
the champions of the earth
the awesome ones
the higher beings
those anointed straight from birth

courage and compassion
with the cunning of a thief
boldness and much confidence
not a thought of disbelief

immortal in our memories
undefeated in our minds
they will leave a lasting footprint
upon the sandy shores of time

history

I asked a man
named history
though odd and strange
his name to me
what past events could help me see
what future things
would come to me.

he looked me straight
into the eye,
his mouth now trickled
with a smile,
and with his arms
he pulled me close,
as my crippling thoughts
then soon arose.

"I'll tell you what
the future holds,
but only if you promise me
you won't forget
I'll always be
lurking back
for all to see.

"for past events
shape future things
but foolish men,
they fail to see
that one cannot
get rid of me
unless he has
the remedy...

"your history is
your destiny
but with God's help
this cannot be."

infinite laws

by the sweat of his brow
he came to see
that such infinite laws
would always be.

and by the toil of his hands
he was reminded of
the mighty hand
that worketh above.

he knew sun would still shine
and the wind would still blow
and those waters would ebb
and flow to and fro.

that seed time and harvest
would not come to an end
that the wonders of history
would repeat soon again.

that the ones whom the world
admired so much
would face many trials
and be tempted as such.

so he made up his mind
to not work quite as hard
but to learn all he could
about the wonders of God.

for his infinite laws
are so fixed in the earth
'twas the beginning of time
that he gave those laws birth.

oppression

power
with mental inferiority
will always lead
to oppression.

power
with mental soundness
remains the path
to effective leadership.

through the fire

I have made it
through the fire
so I won't mess
with the matches
or play
with the smoke
again

agony

"what shall be, and what is,
what shall be, and what is,"
the visionary cries.

don't show me what shall be
when my bleak reality overwhelms me
torn between the future
and the now
the future
and the now
the future
and the now

what shall be
and what is.
what shall be
and what is,
creates agony
in my life.

for my hope
has been deferred
and my heart
has been made sick.
a king in a field
being humbled
by the sheep.

my destiny
put off
has made me hasten
the process
but a blessing too soon
is not a blessing at all.

"what shall be, and what is,
what shall be, and what is,"
the visionary cries.

the agony in my life.

press on

the magnitude
of a man
is measured by
how hard
he presses

future

I peeked into the future
and my life was shown to me.
I saw a noble man,
a gentleman,
all the stuff I'd like to be.

not a hint of any failure,
nor could my sin
at all be found.
my mind was uncorrupted,
chains on my thoughts
had come unbound.

my eyes, they truly glistened,
and my face gave off a glow.
my past, though it was heavy—
look at this smile, you wouldn't know.

so I made a resolution
as my future stared at me:
I will try my best,
to be a better man
until my future
comes to be.

maximizing the maximum

when we maximize the world
but minimize God,
the result is lack of peace,
anxiety.

when we minimize the world,
but maximize God,
the result is true peace.

false dreams

I hoped that I
would be the one
that fame would crown
as number one

I prayed that all
my earthly dreams
would call me up
to greater things

dreams of fortune
and of fame
dreams that all
would know my name

dreams that I
would be the one
the critics tout
as number one

dreams that power
would crown my head
and cause my reach
to swell again

but hope in shallow
earthly things
I know won't stop
the pain it brings

diamonds

a diamond
is a diamond
though it be trampled
on the ground.

its worth
will never falter
though its treatment
be unsound.

though the people
deem it worthless
and some others
curse its name,
its inherent
worth and value
shall forever
be the same.

though it go ragged
through the mud
though it be treated
with all disdain
it will never
end up worthless.

yes, its worth
remains the same.

what's inside

the dream that sits
so deep inside
is a dream that I
just cannot hide.
it haunts my thoughts
each day and night,
it makes me feel
like life's not right.
for to dream and not
have dreams come to be
is the worst of pains
men cannot see.
now my soul knows well
what I must do.
I must take my dreams
and hand them to you.

closer

all the love
I'll ever need
is wrapped up tight
inside of you

so please come close
and I'll untie
the love I need
give it a try

I'll take your comfort
and leave my pain
I know my life
won't be the same

your wrapped-up love
is all I need
to fix this heart
and it won't bleed

it won't bleed
it won't bleed
it won't bleed

the truth

the truth sometimes
is hard to hear.
its words stay ringing
in both our ears.

it never falters,
it never lies.
its words cut deep,
won't compromise.

so tell the truth
just keep things real,
it's all we have
to truly feel.

troubles

when you have troubles,
I am with you.
when you cross rivers,
you will not be hurt.
when you walk through fire,
you will not be burned;
the flames will not hurt you.

draw us near

a bare heart
that beats for you,
a heart that burns by looking
at the man that burns.

let us touch those burning affections,
shed light on the unpossessed areas.
kiss us back to life
and awaken us with your gaze.

for we are infected
with lovesickness
a deep and abounding
lovesickness

draw us near
draw us near
draw us near

these words

I hope these words
will shine right through
the heart that rests
inside of you

I hope these poems
will heal the pain
that years of trauma
have hurt and strained

I hope your heart
will soon be healed
of all the bad
that would not yield

I hope your life
will stand the tests
and shine a light
for all the rest

Ebenezer O. Makinde